THE BEATLES

Edited by Milton Okun

ISBN #: 0-89524-173-0

Contents:

48 All You Need Is Love
10 Can't Buy Me Love
59 Come Together
26 Eight Days A Week
70 Get Back
14 A Hard Day's Night
52 Hello, Goodbye
35 Help!
56 Hey Jude
20 I Feel Fine
17 I Want To Hold Your Hand
62 Let It Be
67 The Long And Winding Road
7 Love Me Do
23 Paperback Writer
40 Penny Lane
3 She Loves You
30 Ticket To Ride
45 We Can Work It Out
38 Yesterday

She Loves You

By JOHN LENNON and PAUL McCARTNEY

Moderately

G6
Em
loves you and you know that can't be bad. Yes, she
Cm6
D
loves you and you know you should be glad. She
G
Em
Bm
D
said you hurt her so, She almost lost her mind. But
know it's up to you, I think it's only fair.
G
Em
Bm
D
now she says she knows You're not the hurting kind. She says she
Pride can hurt you too A-pol-o-gize to her Be-cause she

G6
Em
loves you and you know that can't be bad. Yes, she
Cm6
D
loves you and you know you should be glad, oo! She
Em add G
A7
loves you, yeah, yeah, yeah, She loves you, yeah, yeah, yeah. And with a
Cm6
D+
D7
1. G
love like that you know you should be glad. You

2.
G
Em
Cm6
With a love like that you
D+
D7
G
Em
Cm6
know you should be glad.
With a love like that you
D+
D7
G
Em add G
know you should be glad. Yeah,
yeah, yeah,
Yeah,
much slower
in tempo
C add G
G6
yeah, yeah,
Yeah,
yeah, yeah,
yeah!

Love Me Do

By JOHN LENNON and PAUL McCARTNEY

Moderate rock

*Mixolydian mode, not the Key of C.

Break
please
Love me
G7 C G
1. G7 C
do.
Woh,
love me do.
G
2. G7 C G
me do.
D G7
Some - one to love,
some - bod - y
new.

D
G7
Break
Some - one to love, some - one like you.
G7
C add G
G7
C add G
Love, love me do, you know I love you, I'll
G7
C add G
Break
al - ways be true, so please Love me
G7
C
G
G7
C
G
After repeat, D. C. and fade
do. Woh, love me do.

Can't Buy Me Love

By JOHN LENNON and PAUL McCARTNEY

C
G
makes you feel al - right. 'Cause I don't care too
got I'll give to you. 'Cause I don't care too
F7
Break
1.
C
much for mon - ey, for mon - ey can't buy me love. I'll
much for mon - ey, for mon - ey can't buy me love.
2.3.
C
Em
Am
Can't buy me love, ev -
C
Em
- 'ry - bod - y tells me so. Can't buy me love,

Am
Dm7
G
no no no
no!
C
Say you don't need no dia - mond rings and I'll be sat - is - fied,
F7
C
Tell me that you want the kind of things that mon - ey just can't buy.
G
F7
Break
To Coda
I don't care too much for mon - ey,

F7
C
D. S. al Coda
mon - ey can't buy me love.
(Scream)
Coda
F7
C
Em
mon - ey can't buy me love.
Can't buy me love
Am
Em
Am
love
can't buy me love.
Dm7
G
C

A Hard Day's Night

By JOHN LENNON and PAUL McCARTNEY

C
D
get home to you I find the thing that you do will make me
love to come home 'Cause when I get you a - lone you know I'll
G
C9
To Coda
1. G
feel al - right. 2. You know I
be O. K.
2. G
Bm
Em
When I'm home ev - 'ry - thing seems to be al -
Bm
G
right, When I'm home

Em
C
D
D. S. al Coda
feel - ing you hold - ing me tight, tight, yeah, 3. It's been a
Coda
G
C9
You know I feel al - right,
G
CaddD
N. C.
You know I feel al - right.
Ped al fine
Repeat and fade

I Want To Hold Your Hand

By JOHN LENNON and PAUL McCARTNEY

G Em C D 1.G 2.G
hand, I want to hold your hand. Oh,
hand, I want to hold your hand.
Dm7 G C Am Dm7
And when I touch you I feel hap-py in-side. It's such a
more smoothly
G C D C D C D
feel-ing that my love I can't hide, I can't hide, I can't hide!
G
Yeah, you got that
Yeah, you got that
as before

D
Em
Bm
G
some-thing I think you'll un - der - stand. When I say that
some-thing I think you'll un - der - stand. When I feel that
D
Em
Bm
C
D
some-thing, I want to hold your hand,
some-thing, I want to hold your
G
Em
1. C
D
G
2. C
D
hand, I want to hold your hand.
I want to hold your
B7
C
D
C
G
hand, I want to hold your hand.

I Feel Fine

By JOHN LENNON and PAUL McCARTNEY

Bright rock

*Mixolydian mode, not Key of C.

C
G7
I'm in love with her and I feel fine. (repeat to 2nd lyric)
I'm in love with her and I feel fine. (continue)
I'm in love with her and I feel fine. (continue)
G
3fr
Bm
C
D
I'm so glad that she's my lit - tle girl.
G
3fr
Bm
C
D
She's so glad she's tell - ing all the world that her
G7
ba - by buys her things, you know, he buys her dia - mond rings

D
— you know, — she said so.
C
G7
To Coda
D. S. al Coda
She's in love — with me and I — feel — fine. —
Coda
G7
D
C
She's in love — with me and I — feel — fine. —
G7
N. C.
Repeat and fade

Paperback Writer

By JOHN LENNON and PAUL McCARTNEY

C
G7
want to be a pa - per - back writ - er, pa - per - back
want to be a pa - per - back writ - er, pa - per - back
writ - er. It's the dirt - y sto - ry of a dirt - y man, and his
writ - er. If you real - ly like it you can have the rights, it could
cling - ing wife does - n't un - der - stand. His son is work - ing for the
make a mil - lion for you o - ver - night. If you must re - turn it you can
Dai - ly Mail; It's a stead - y job but he wants to be a pa - per - back
send it here, But I need a break and I want to be a pa - per - back

C
G7
writ - er, paper-back writ - er.
writ - er, paper-back writ - er.
N. C.
Pa - per - back writ - er, writ - er.
Pa - per - back writ - er.
G7
Repeat and fade
Pa - per-back writ - er.

Eight Days A Week

By JOHN LENNON and PAUL McCARTNEY

Bm
E
D
Hold me, love me. I ain't got noth - in' but
E
G
D
love, babe, eight days a week.
3
A
Bm
Eight days a week, I love
3
E
you. Eight days a week is

G6
A
D
not e - nough to show I care.
Ooh I need your
Love you ev - 'ry
f
E
G
D
love, babe, guess you know it's true.
day, girl, al - ways on my mind.
E
G
Hope you need my love, babe, just like I need you.
One thing I can say, girl, love you all the time.
D
Bm
G6
Hold me, love me.

Bm
E
D
Hold me,
love me.
I ain't got noth - in' but
E
G
D
love, babe,
eight days a week.
3
G
D
G
D
Eight days a week.
Eight days a week.
3
3
D
E/D
G/D
D

Ticket To Ride

By JOHN LENNON and PAUL McCARTNEY

*Actually a slide from G♭ to G♮.

C7
D♭7
don't know why she's rid - in' so high, she ought - ta
D
E♭
think twice; she ought - ta do right by me. Be -
C7
D♭7
fore she gets to say - in' good - bye she ought - ta
D
E♭
think twice, she ought-ta do right by me.
1. I
2. She

G
A♭
think I'm gon - na be sad, I think it's to - day
said that liv - ing with me is bring - in' her down
yeah! The girl that's driv - ing me mad
yeah! For she would nev - er be free
Am7
B♭m7
D7
E♭7
is go - ing a - way.
when I was a - round.
Yeah! Oh,
Em
Fm
C7
D♭7
she's got a tick - et to ride,

Em
Fm
C
D♭
She's got a tick - et to ri - hi - hide,
Em
Fm
D7
E♭7
She's got a tick - et to ride, but she don't care!
1. G
A♭
I
2. G
A♭
G
A♭
Falsetto
Repeat and fade
My ba - by don't care!

Help!

By JOHN LENNON and PAUL McCARTNEY

F♯m
2fr
D
G
A
I nev - er need - ed an - y - bod - y's help in an - y way. _
My in - de - pen-dence seems _ to van - ish in the haze. _
C♯m
4fr
But now these days are gone, _ I'm not so self - as - sured,
But ev - 'ry now and then _ I feel so in - se - cure,
F♯m
2fr
D
G
A
Now I find I've changed my mind, I've o - pened up the doors. _
I know that I just need you like I've nev - er done be - fore. _
Bm
Bm/A
Help me if you can, _ I'm feel - ing down,
And I do _

G
G/F♯
appreciate you being 'round.
E7
Help me get my feet back on the ground. Won't you
A
Chords tacet
please please help me?
1.2.
A
3. F♯m
2fr
A
A6
Help me, Help me! Oo.

Yesterday

By JOHN LENNON and PAUL McCARTNEY

F A11 A7 Dm C B♭ Dm/A Gm C
say. I said some-thing wrong, now I long for yes-ter-
F Em7 A7
day. Yes-ter-day, love was such an eas-y
Dm Dm/C B♭ C F C/E
game to play Now I need a place to hide a-way Oh
Dm G B♭ F F/C G/B B♭ F
I be-lieve in yes-ter-day. Mm mm mm mm mm.

Penny Lane

By JOHN LENNON and PAUL McCARTNEY

A F♯m Am Am/F♯
B G♯m Bm Bm/G♯
dren laugh at him be-hind his back. And the bank-er nev-er wears a "mac"
er sit-ting wait-ing for a trim. And then the fire - man rush - es in
Am/F E7/4 D
Bm/G F♯7/4 E
N. C.
in the pour - ing rain, ver-y strange! Pen-ny
from the pour - ing rain, ver-y strange! Pen-ny
G G/B C
A A/C♯ D
Lane is in my ears and in my eyes,
Lane is in my ears and in my eyes,
G G/B
(Harmony)
A A/C♯
Wet be-neath the blue sub-ur-ban skies
There be-neath the blue sub-ur-ban skies

C
D
To Coda
N.C.
A
B
F♯m
G♯m
I sit. And mean-while back in Pen-ny Lane there is a fire-man with an
I sit. And (to Coda)
Bm7
C♯m7
E7 4
F♯7 4
A
B
F♯m
G♯m
hour glass, And in his pock - et is a por-trait of the
Am
Bm
Am/F♯
Bm/G♯
Am/F
Bm/G
Queen. He likes to keep his fire en-gine clean; It's a clean
E7 4
F♯7 4
A
B
F♯m
G♯m
ma-chine!
(Piccolo Trpt. Solo)

Bm7
C♯m7
E
F♯
A
B
F♯m
G♯m
Am
Bm
Am/F♯
Bm/G♯
Am/F
Bm/G
E7 4
F♯7 4
D
E
G
A
G/B
A/C♯
Pen - ny Lane is in my ears and in my eyes,
C
D
G
A
A four of fish

G/B
C
A/C#
D
N. C.
D. S. al Coda
and fin - ger pies in sum - mer. Mean - while back be - hind the
Coda
N. C.
A
B
A/C#
B/D#
3
mean - while back. . . Pen - ny Lane is in my ears and in my eyes.
D
E
Trpt.
A
B
There be - neath the blue
A/C#
B/D#
D
E
A
B
3
3
sub - ur - ban skies Pen - ny Lane.

We Can Work It Out

By JOHN LENNON and PAUL McCARTNEY

Bm
Bm/A
Bm/G
Life is ver - y short and there's no time
F♯sus4
F♯
Bm
Bm/A
for fuss - ing and fight - ing, my friend.
Bm/G
Bm/F♯
Bm
Bm/A
I have al - ways thought that it's a crime
Bm/G
F♯sus4
F♯
Bm
Bm/A
so I will ask you once a -

Bm/G
Bm/F#
D
Dsus4
D
gain. ___
Try to see it my way,
Dsus4
CaddD
D
Dsus4
D
on-ly time will tell if I am right or I am wrong.
While you see it your way
Dsus4
CaddD
D
there's a chance that we might fall a-part be-fore too long.
G
D
G
Asus4
A
D
G6/D
D
We can work it out,
we can work it out. ___

All You Need Is Love

By JOHN LENNON and PAUL McCARTNEY

G
D/F♯
Em
1. There's noth - ing you can do that can't be done
2. Noth - ing you can make that can't be made
3. Noth - ing you can know that is - n't known
Noth - ing you can sing that can't be sung.
No one you can save that can't be saved.
Noth - ing you can see that is - n't shown.
D7/A
D7
Noth-ing you can say but you can learn how to play the game It's
Noth-ing you can do but you can learn how to be you in time It's
No-where you can be that is - n't where you're meant to be It's
eas - y
eas - y
eas - y
N. C.
Chorus: (last time, repeat and fade)
A7sus4
All you need is love

D7
G
A7sus4
all you need is love,
D7
G
B7
Em
G
all you need is love,
love,
C
D9
G
G
D/F#
love is all you need.
Love love
mf
Em
G
D/F#
Em
love
love love
love

D7/A
G
D/F♯
D9
D7
Love love love
N. C.
G
A7sus4
D7
All you need is love,
G
A7sus4
D7
G
B7
all you need is love,
all you need is love,
Em
G
C
D9
G
D.S. and fade on Chorus
love,
love is all you need.

Hello, Goodbye

By JOHN LENNON and PAUL McCARTNEY

Moderato

C/A
C/G
I don't know
F
why you say good-bye,
Bb
I say hel-lo.
C
F
I say high
You say yes
C
You say low
I say no
G7
You say why and
You say stop and
Am
I say I don't know
I say go go go
G7
Am
Oh
Oh no
G

G7
F/G
C
C/B
You say good-bye and I say hel-lo hel-lo hel-lo
C/A
C/G
F
A♭
I don't know why you say good-bye I say hel-lo
C
C/B
C/A
C/G
F
B♭
To Coda
hel-lo hel-lo I don't know why you say good-bye I say hel-lo
C
F
C
Solo
Why why why

G7
Am
G
D. S. al Coda
why why why do you say goodbye goodbye
Coda
C
C/B
C/A
C/G
Hel - lo hel - lo I don't know
F
A♭
A♭/G
why you say good - bye I say hel - lo
A♭/F♯
A♭/F
C
C
Repeat and fade
Hel - lo Hel - lo he - ba hel - lo - a

Hey Jude

By JOHN LENNON and PAUL McCARTNEY

D F G B♭ D F
get her. The min-ute you let her un-der your skin, then you be-gin
get her. Re-mem-ber to let her in-to your heart, then you can start
A7 C7 D F D7 F7
to make it bet-ter. And an-y time you feel the pain
to make it bet-ter. So let it out and let it in
G B♭ Em7 Gm7 A7 C7
Hey Jude, re-frain, don't car-ry the world up-on your shoul-
Hey Jude, be-gin, you're wait-ing for some-one to per-form
D F D7 F7 G B♭
ders. For well you know that it's a fool who plays it cool.
with. And don't you know that it's just you Hey Jude, you'll do.

Em7 A7 D
Gm7 C7 F
By mak - ing his world a lit - tle cold - er. Da da da
The move - ment you need is on your shoul - der. Da da da
D7 A7
F7 C7
1. 2. D. S. al Coda
da da da da da da. Hey
da da da da da da. Hey
Coda
A7 D
C7 F
to make it bet - ter, bet-ter, bet-ter, bet-ter, bet-ter, bet-ter, Oh
D C G D
F E♭ B♭ F
Repeat and fade
Da da da da da da da da da da da Hey Jude.

Come Together

By JOHN LENNON and PAUL McCARTNEY

Moderately slow, with a double-time feeling

G7
N.C.
Dm7
Got to be a jok - er, He just do what he please.
Dm7
He wear no shoe - shine, He got toe jam foot - ball, He got
He Bag Pro - duc - tion, He got wal - rus gum - boot, He got
He roll - er coast - er, He got ear - ly warn - ing, He got
mon - key fin - ger, He shoot Co - ca Co - la, He say,
O - no side - board, He one spi - nal crack - er, He got
Mud - dy Wa - ter, He one Mo - jo fil - ter, He say,

*Instrumental omitted.

Let It Be

By JOHN LENNON and PAUL McCARTNEY

Am G F C G
stand-ing right in front of me
Speak-ing words of wis-dom, Let it
F C/E Dm7 C Am G
be.
Let it be, let it be, let it be,
Let it be, let it be, let it be,
f
F C G
let it be,
let it be,
Whis-per words of wis-dom, Let it be.
Whis-per words of wis-dom, Let it be.
F C/E Dm7 C C G
2. And when the bro-ken-heart-ed peo-ple
4. And when the night is cloud-y there is

Am G F C G
liv - ing in the world a - gree There will be an an - swer, Let it
still a light that shines on me Shine un - til to - mor - row, Let it
F C/E Dm7 C G
be. For though they may be part - ed there is
be. I wake up to the sound of mu - sic
Am G F C G
still a chance that they will see There will be an an - swer, Let it
Moth - er Mar - y comes to me Speak - ing words of wis - dom, Let it
F C/E Dm7 C Am G
be. Let it be, let it be, let it be,
be.
f

F C G
let it be, There will be an an - swer, Let it be.
F C/E Dm7 C G Am G
Let it be, let it be, let it be,
F C G
let it be,
To Coda
Whis - per words of wis - dom, let it be.
There will be an an - swer, let it be.
F C Dm7 C F Em Dm7 C B♭ F/A
f

D. S. al Coda
G F C F C G F C
Coda F C/E Dm7 C Am G
Let it be, let it be, let it be,
F C G
let it be. Whisper words of wis-dom, let it be.
F C/E Dm7 C F Em Dm7 C B♭ F/A G F C

The Long And Winding Road

By JOHN LENNON and PAUL McCARTNEY

2. C
Eb
C/G
Eb/Bb
F
Ab
C/E
Eb/G
Dm7
Fm7
G7
Bb7
way. Man-y times_ I've been a-lone_ and man-y times_ I've cried,
C/G
Eb/Bb
F
Ab
C/E
Eb/G
Dm7
Fm7
Am
Cm
Em
Gm
An-y-way_you'll nev-er know_ the man-y ways_ I've tried. And still they lead me back_
G9sus4
Bb9sus4
C
Eb
C/Bb
Eb/Db
F
Ab
_ to the long_ wind-ing road,_
C/E
Eb/G
Am
Cm
Dm7
Fm7
G7
Bb7
You left me stand-ing here, a long, long time a-go,_

C7sus4 C7 F C/E Am Am7
E♭7sus4 E♭7 A♭ E♭/G Cm Cm7
Don't leave me wait - ing here,
Don't keep me wait - ing here,
Dm7 G7 C C/G F
Fm7 B♭7 E♭ E♭/B♭ A♭
To Coda
lead me to your door.
Solo
C/E Dm7 C/G F C/E Dm7
E♭/G Fm7 E♭/B♭ A♭ E♭/G Fm7
D. S. al Coda
But
Coda
C G9sus4 Cmaj7
E♭ B♭9sus4 E♭maj7
door.
Yeah, yeah, yeah, yeah.
f

Get Back

By JOHN LENNON and PAUL McCARTNEY

D
- son, Ar - i - zo - na, for some Cal - i - for - nia grass.
she's got it com - ing, But she gets it while she can.
A
A7
Am7
Get back!
Get back!
A7
Am7
D
Get back to where you once be - longed.
A
G/A
D/A
A7
Am7
Get back!
Get back!

A7
Am7
D
1.
A
Get back to where you once be - longed. (Get back, Jo Jo)
2.
Chords tacet
Repeat and fade
A
Get back, Loretta, your momma's waitin' for you
Wearin' her high heel shoes and a low neck sweater.
Get back home, Loretta.
D
A
G/A
D/A